John Fisher

An illustrated record of national gold, silver and bronze medal designs, models, drawings, etc.

Edited and compiled by John Fisher, headmaster, Kensington school of science and

art, Birstol

John Fisher

An illustrated record of national gold, silver and bronze medal designs, models, drawings, etc.
Edited and compiled by John Fisher, headmaster, Kensington school of science and art, Birstol

ISBN/EAN: 9783742879325

Manufactured in Europe, USA, Canada, Australia, Japa

Cover: Foto ©Andreas Hilbeck / pixelio.de

Manufactured and distributed by brebook publishing software
(www.brebook.com)

John Fisher

An illustrated record of national gold, silver and bronze medal designs, models, drawings, etc.

NATIONAL
COMPETITIONS
1896-97

AN ILLUSTRATED
RECORD

OF NATIONAL GOLD, SILVER AND
BRONZE MEDAL DESIGNS,
MODELS, DRAWINGS, ETC.

EDITED AND COMPILED BY JOHN
FISHER, HEADMASTER, KENSINGTON
SCHOOL OF SCIENCE AND ART,
BRISTOL

London:
CHAPMAN & HALL, LTD.
1899.

Modelled Design for a Fireplace
at the Side of a Room.

ERNEST G. GILLICK,
NOTTINGHAM.

An Illustrated Record of the National Competitions
1896-97.

THE education of the Art Student is probably the most difficult of all tasks to undertake, as so much attraction is offered to the immature mind by the restless and ever-changing fashion, the incessant craving for that which is novel rather than that which is artistic, and the aggressive expression of opinion and judgment by those who have not taken the trouble to cultivate a close acquaintance with the laws of art. The student is often led into error, and in some cases, I may say, forced into error in consequence of the necessity of a reliable text-book to which he may refer with confidence, for his artistic guidance. Books are only good as far as the student is ready for them, and the best of teaching frequently fails in producing good results, through the lack of practical demonstration. In placing this illustrated record of the National Competitions, 1896-7, before the public, I am guided by the necessity which exists of providing the Art Student with matter for thought and with a practical demonstration of the thoughts and work of others, and further with a guide to what the examiners of the Department of Science and Art require, if the student desires to obtain success under their examination. As the progress of a life is best judged by comparison with the life of others, this book should prove of inestimable value to students in that all examples contained herein, are the works of students executed under conditions of considerable similitude, though probably varying in minor details, and which have been awarded Gold, Silver and Bronze Medals, or National Book Prizes. The master and teacher will also herein, find assistance of a most valuable character in the form of suggestion, both in point of design, method and execution, and a reference of work done, and a spur to future efforts.

The designer will probably benefit even more largely than the others, as the numerous illustrations are all taken from works which have received the critical approbation of expert examiners, and have been proved by the trying ordeal of competitive comparison with large numbers of works of a similar class, thus affording a guarantee of the worth of each example.

The manufacturer, in whose hands is placed so much power in the spreading of artistic taste and knowledge, will herein find guidance and suggestion as to the direction of public taste, moreover the exposition of such a large and varied collection of applied art work must by its completeness prove an incentive to efforts on his part to help forward in a general sense, the attempt which is being made so energetically for the advancement of higher artistic productions. The attention of the general public, which is so monopolised by the hurry and bustle of commercial enterprise as to prevent visits being paid to the annual exhibitions at South Kensington Museum, has herein an opportunity of becoming at once cognizant with the value of the applied art teaching of our country—value which is not in any way confined to the artistic side only, but which has a decided commercial interest, and which carries with it a prophetic character as to the ultimate result in the race for world-wide supremacy in industrial art and art productions. For the large army of amateurs who are merely content to dabble in Art, or Arts and Crafts, a rich fund of suggestion and instruction is at once provided. The academic character of a number of the examples should act as a guide, and prove a source of inspiration.

With the foregoing reasons for placing this work before the general public, I am content to await judgment as to its fitness. Criticism on all the examples would be much too tedious to be of service. Criticism on a few individual examples would be too invidious to be politic, therefore I leave it to others.

JOHN FISHER.

Kensington Government School of
Science and Art,
Bristol.

INDEX OF ILLUSTRATIONS.

NOTE.

NATICNAL
COMPETITIONS
1899-97

Design for Printed Silk.

SILVER MEDAL.

SILVER MEDAL. Design for Wall Tiles. ARTHUR FORD,
MACCLESFIELD.

4

BRONZE MEDAL.

Design for Woven Silk Hanging.
ETHEL POPPLETON.
HARTWIN STR., LEICESTER.

NATIONAL BOOK PRIZE.

Design for Silk Hanging.
ERNEST G. GILLACK,
NOTTINGHAM.

Bronze Medal.   Design for Wall Tiles.   William Hawhorn, Macclesfield.

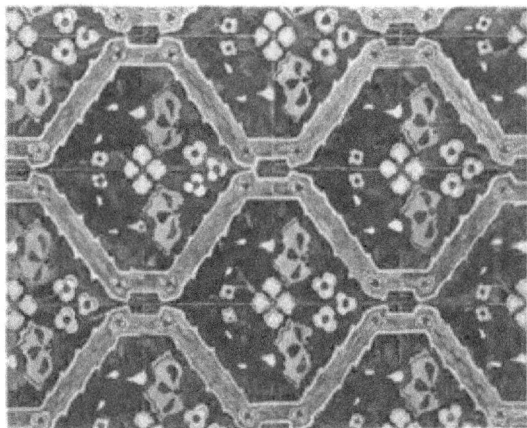

Bronze Medal.   Design for Tiles.   H. A. Wright, Bradford (Technical School).

Design for Damask Table Cloth.

John G. Hardy,
Royal College of Art.

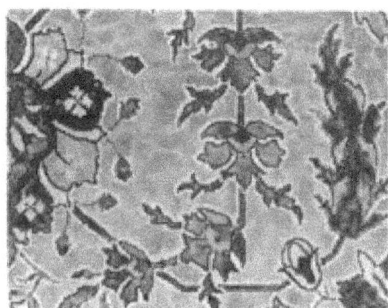

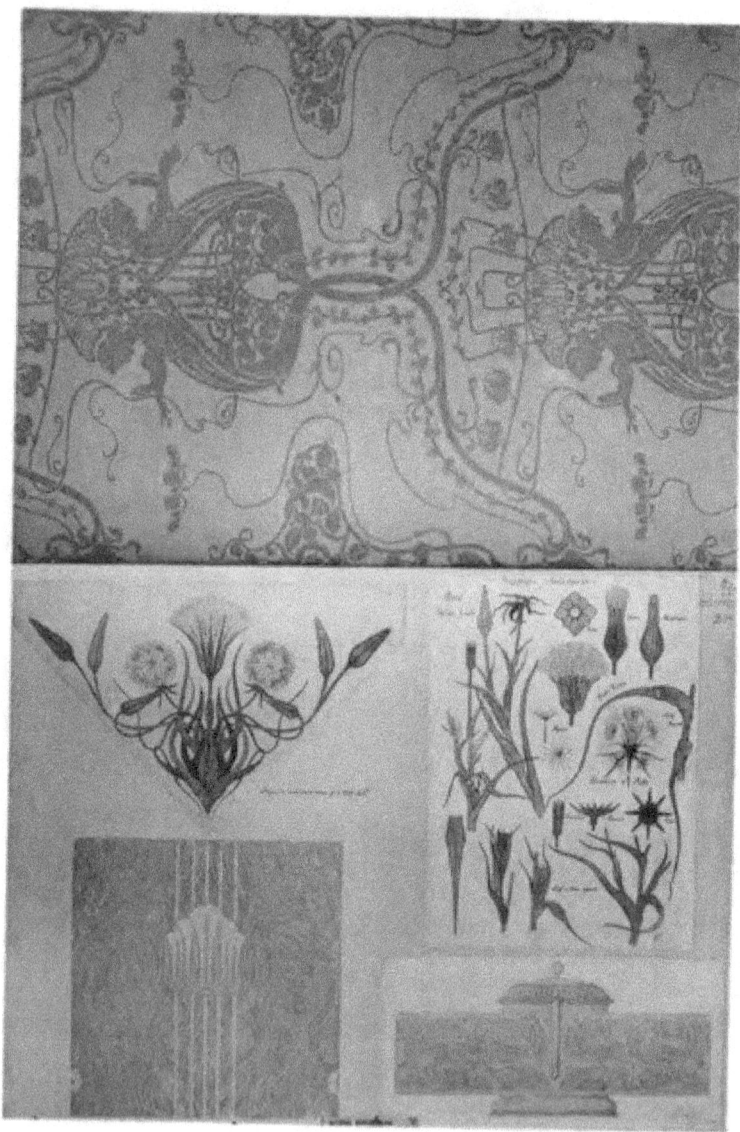

Design for a Wall Paper.

Designs based on a Flowering Plant.

Lewis C. Radcliffe.
Royal College of Art.

Frank Geonges,
Brighton.

Bronze Medal. Silver Medal.

Design for Axminster Carpet.

BRONZE MEDAL FOR SET.

JOSEPH M. SADLER, GLASGOW.

BRONZE MEDAL.   Design for a Ceiling Paper.   PHILIP CONNARD;
ROYAL COLLEGE OF ART.

BRONZE MEDAL.   Design for a Ceiling Paper.   WM. PARKINSON,
ROYAL COLLEGE OF ART.

Design for Silk Hanging.

12

Design for a Lace Collar.

Design for a Lace Collar.

BRONZE MEDAL.   Design for a Lace Flounce and Trimming.   ALICE JACOB. DUBLIN.

BRONZE MEDAL.   Design for a Lace Fan Cover.   ALICE JACOB. DUBLIN.

14

GERTRUDE CHAPMAN.
DOVER.

Designs for Lace.

SILVER MEDAL.

Design for Crochet Insertion and Borders.

Design for a Lace Curtain.

SILVER MEDAL.　　Design for Wall Decoration.　　MARY WATSON, NEWCASTLE-ON-TYNE
DURHAM COLLEGE OF SCIENCE.

BRONZE MEDAL.　　Design for a Panel.　　HARRY A. PAYNE,
BIRMINGHAM.

Design for the Decoration of an Overmantel.

Designs for Book Illustrations.

HAROLD E. H. NELSON.
LAMBETH.

SILVER MEDAL.

SILVER MEDAL.　Designs for Title Pages.　GEORGE MONTAGUE ELLWOOD, HOLLOWAY.

BRONZE MEDAL.　Designs for Book Illustrations.　HENRY M. BROCK, CAMBRIDGE.

R13287

Designs based on a Flowering Plant.

Designs based on a Flowering Plant.

23

Design based on a Flowering Plant.

BRONZE MEDAL.

HERBERT C. OAKLEY.
ROYAL COLLEGE OF ART.

BRONZE MEDAL.

Design based on a Flowering Plant.

ARTHUR H. HAYES.
LEICESTER (HASTINGS ST.)

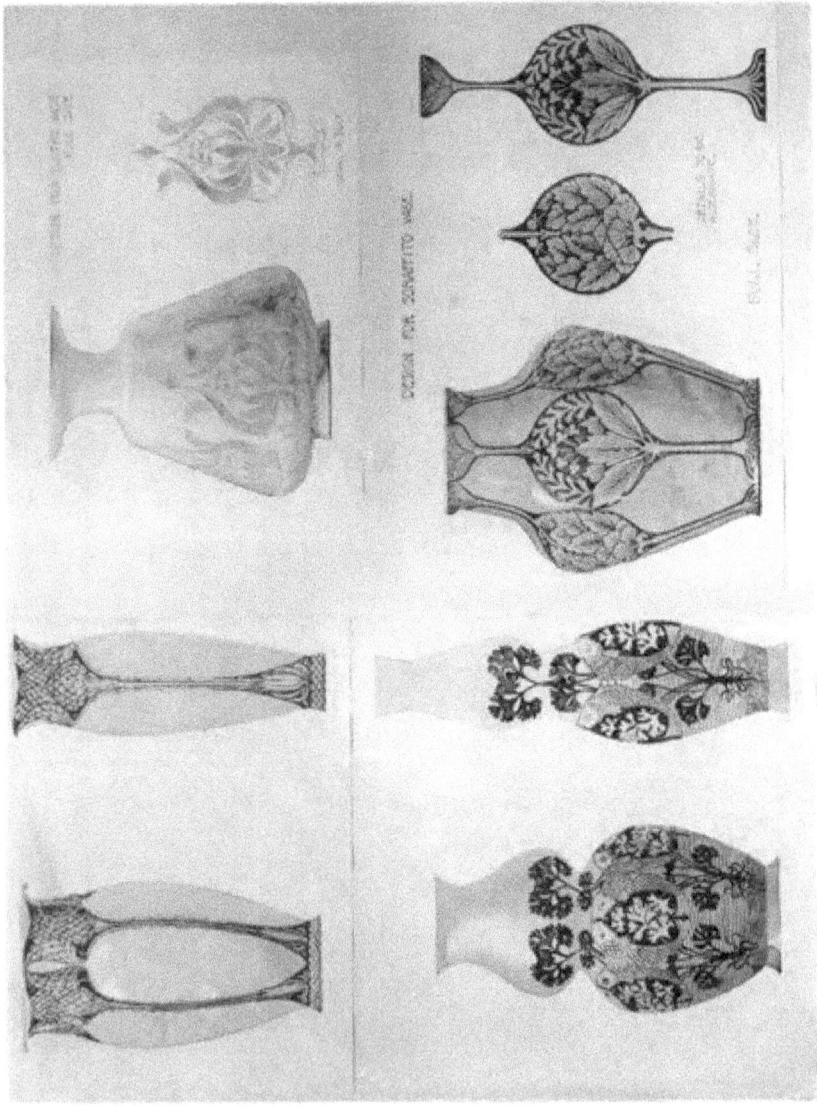

Designs for Sgraffito Vases.

KATE ROBERTS,
NEW CROSS.

BAGNER MEARS.

THE PIED PIPER OF HAMELIN.

Bronze
Medal.
Design for an Illustration. ALICE B. GREI,
LAMBETH.

SILVER Medal. Designs for Coal Boxes and Coal Scuttle. ARTHUR H. BAYER,
LEICESTER.

Analysis of Flowers.

Silver Medal.

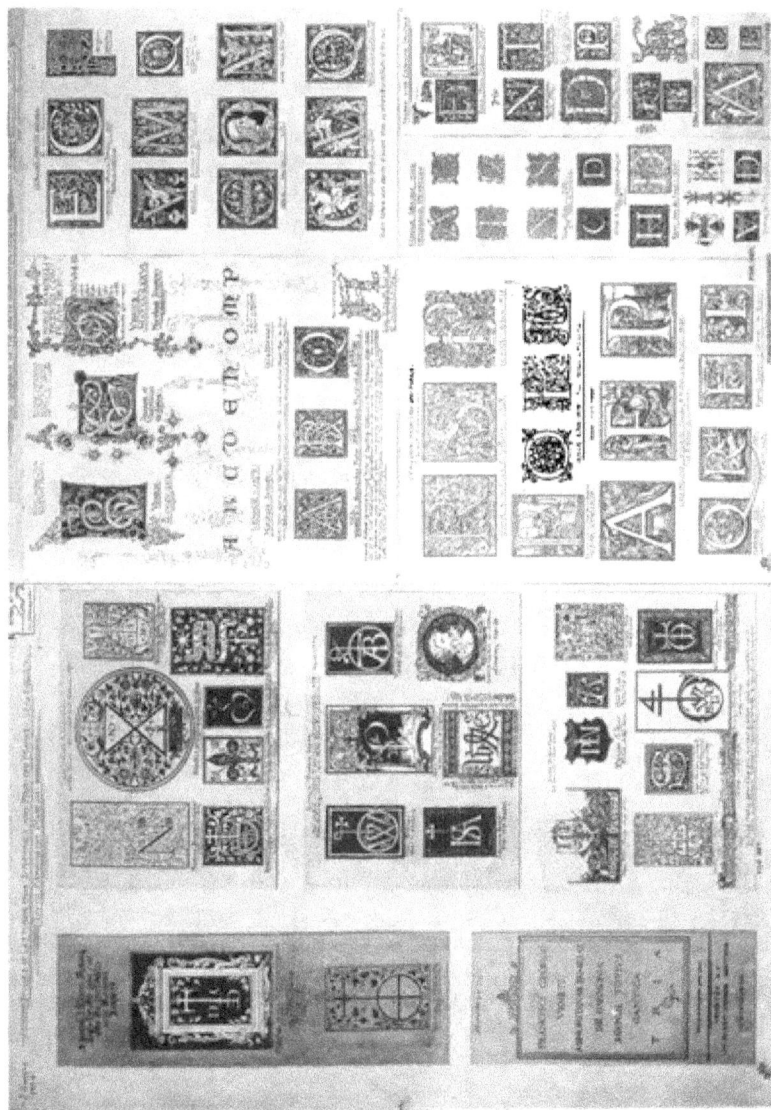

Studies for Historic Styles of Ornament.

WILLIAM HENRY LONG,
ROYAL COLLEGE OF ART

SILVER MEDAL.

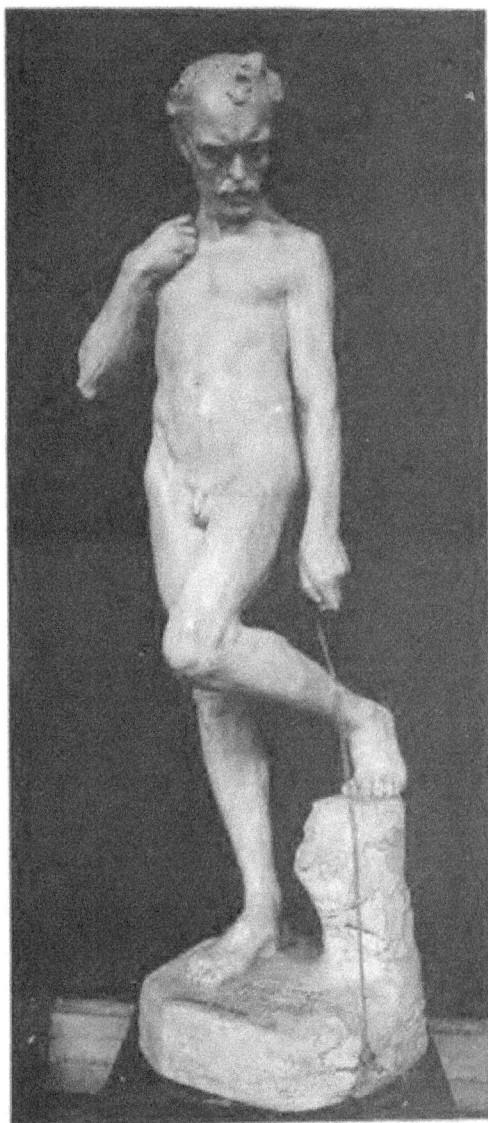

GOLD MEDAL. Model of Figure from the Nude. WILLIAM JAMES MCLEAN, ROYAL COLLEGE OF ART.

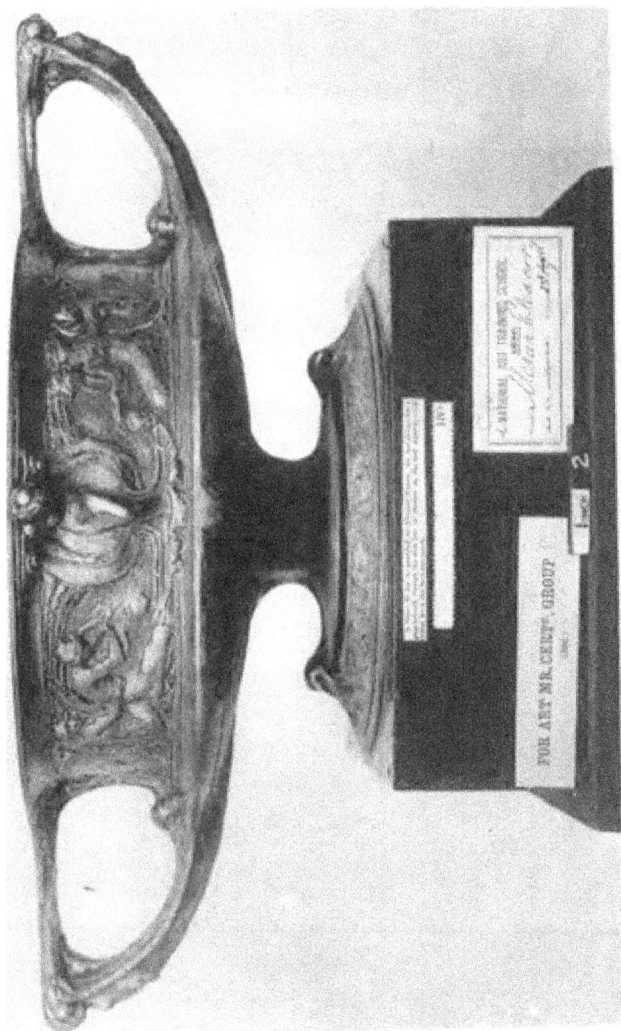

Modelled Design for a Punch Bowl.

Silver Medal.

Eleanor Mercer.
Royal College of Art.

SILVER MEDAL. **Modelled Designs for Memorial Tablet, Medallion and Panel.** SIDNEY J. LEGG, WOLVERHAMPTON.

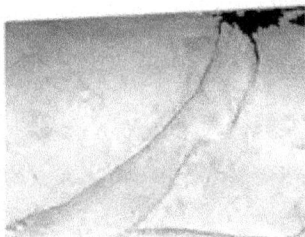

BRONZE MEDAL. **Modelled Design for** MORTIMER J. BROWN, **a Monument.** ROYAL COLLEGE OF ART.   BRONZE MEDAL. **Modelled Design for a Decorative Column.** JANE M. TWISS, ROYAL COLLEGE OF ART.

BRONZE MEDAL.
Modelled Design
for a Pilaster.
FLORENCE H. STULR.

BRONZE MEDAL.

Modelled Design
for a Sun-Dial in Bronze.

ALBERT T. ROBERTS,
LANCASTER (HASTINGS ST.)

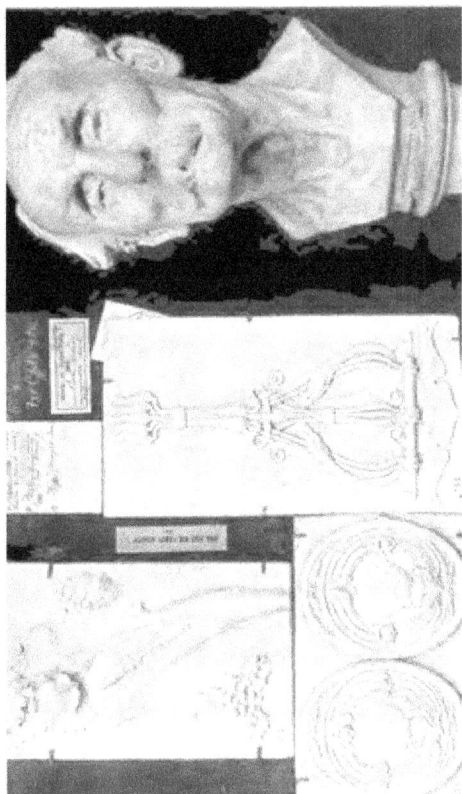

BRONZE MEDAL.   KATHERINE WALLIS.
ROYAL COLLEGE OF ART.
Model of Drapery arranged on the Living Model.

BRONZE MEDAL.   Model of Drapery.   JULIA BARRE.
ROYAL COLLEGE OF ART.

SILVER MEDAL. **Modelled Design based on the Vegetable Marrow.** CHARLES ANDREWS SHEEMAN, KENSINGTON SCHOOL OF ART, BRISTOL.

SILVER MEDAL. **Modelled Design based on the Parsnip.** TRACY TRATMAN, KENSINGTON SCHOOL OF ART, BRISTOL.

OVER THE DOOR OF A WALKING HOSPITAL.

SILVER MEDAL.   Modelled Design for Sprandrils.   JANE M. TWISS, ROYAL COLLEGE OF ART.

BRONZE MEDAL.   Design of a Wall Fountain.   JOHN G. HANDY,
ROYAL COLLEGE OF ART.

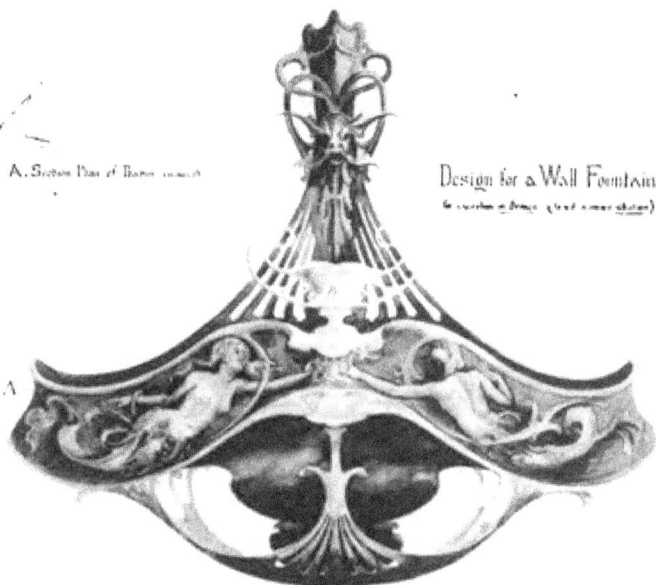

A. Section Plan of Basin

Design for a Wall Fountain.

HONORARY AWARD

DESIGNS FOR METAL DOOR FITTINGS

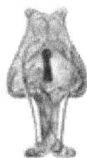

SILVER MEDAL.   Design for Metal Door Fittings.   H. SPENCER STRONGQUIST,
ROYAL COLLEGE OF ART.

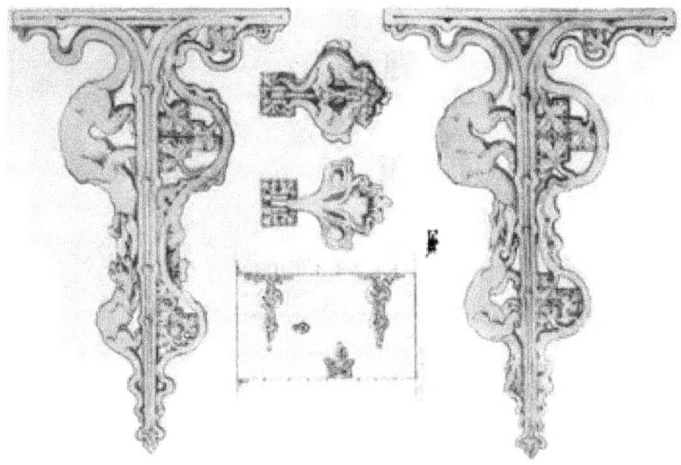

Designs for Hinges and Knocker to be Cast in Bronze.

Philip W. Smith. Manchester.

Bronze Medal.

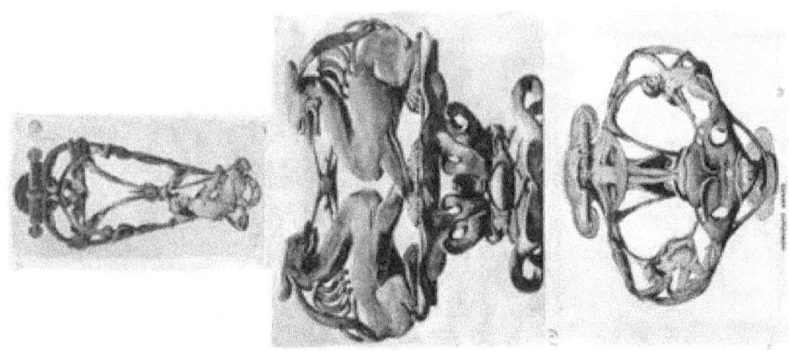

Silver Medal.

Herbert C. Oakley. Royal College of Art.

Designs for Metal Work.

Design for a Hanging Sign. GAMBLE S. LEMAXIE. KINGSTON SCHOOL. BRISTOL.

NATIONAL BOOK PRIZE.

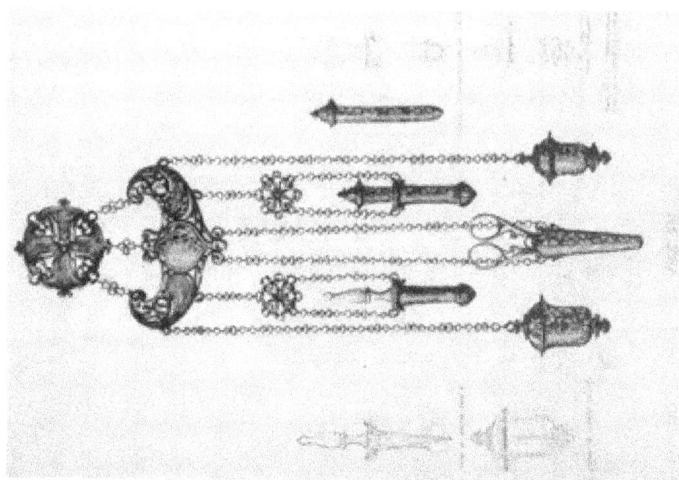

Design for a Chatelaine. ALICE WAINWRIGHT. SHEFFIELD.

BRONZE MEDAL.

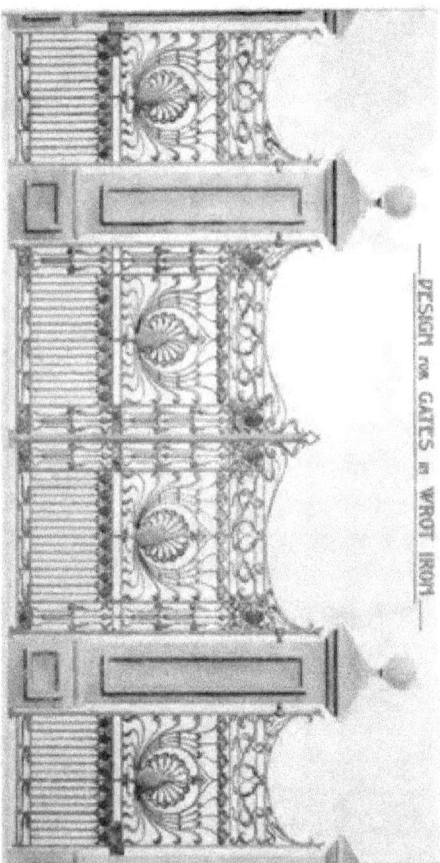

Design for Wrought Iron Gates.

SILVER MEDAL.

ARTHUR H. SMITH, WOLVERHAMPTON.

BRONZE MEDAL.

PHILIP CONNARD, ROYAL COLLEGE OF ART.

Design for a Finger and Lock Plate.

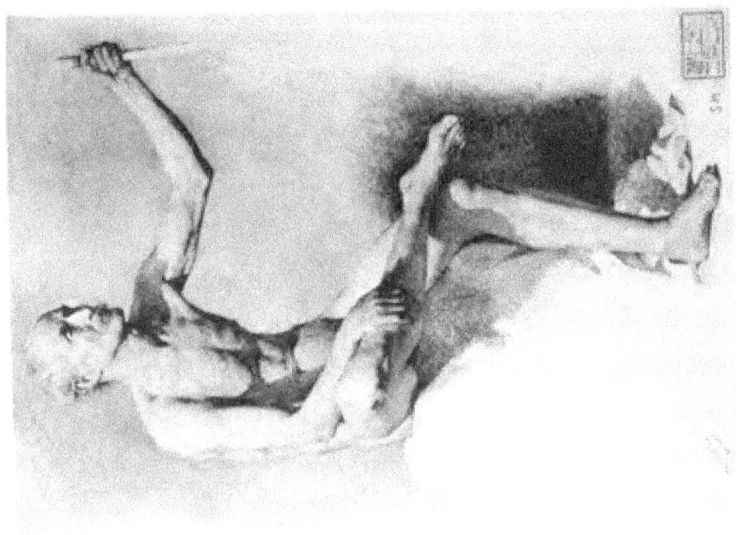

Silver Medal   Chalk Drawing from the Nude.   Wm. X. M. Orpen. Dublin.

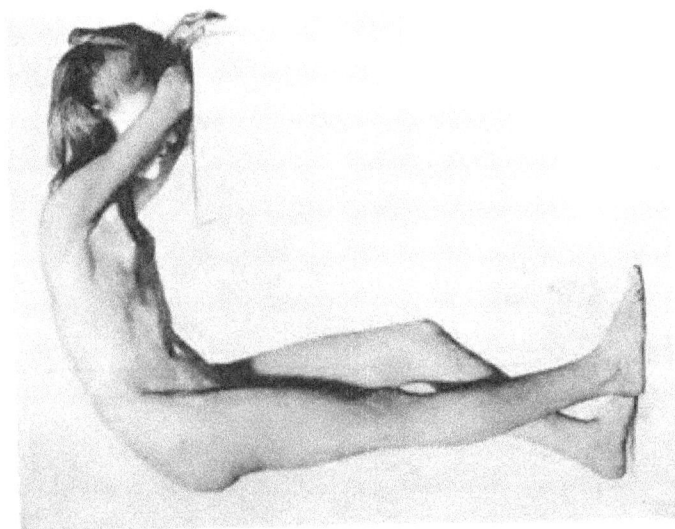

Silver Medal   Chalk Drawing from the Nude   Arthur A. Dixon. Holloway

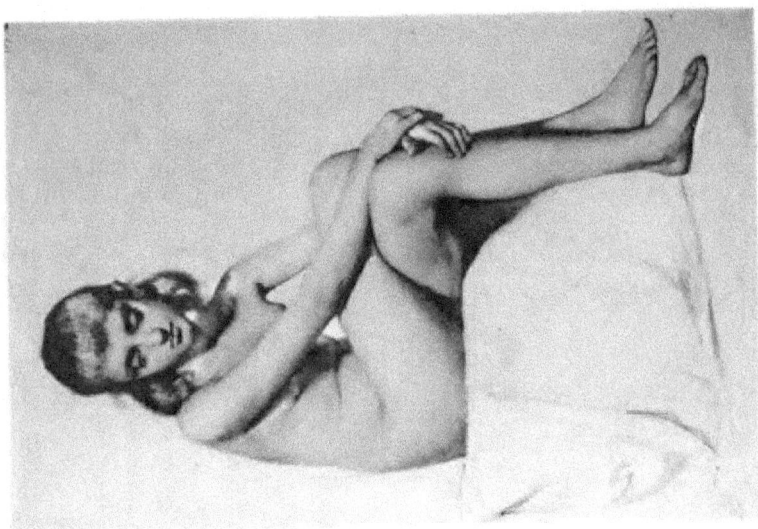

ARTHUR AUGUSTUS DIXON, HOLLOWAY.

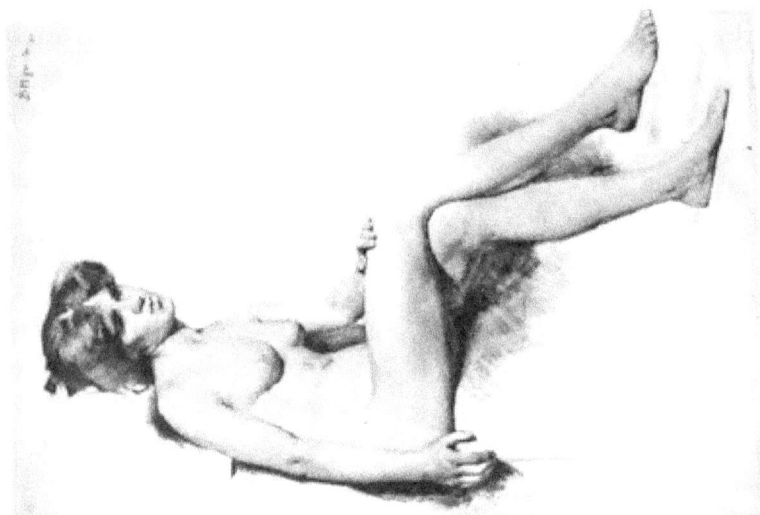

BRONZE MEDAL.

Chalk Drawings of Figures from the Nude.

47

SILVER MEDAL. **Chalk Drawing of a Laocoon.** HERBERT C. OAKLEY.
ROYAL COLLEGE OF ART.

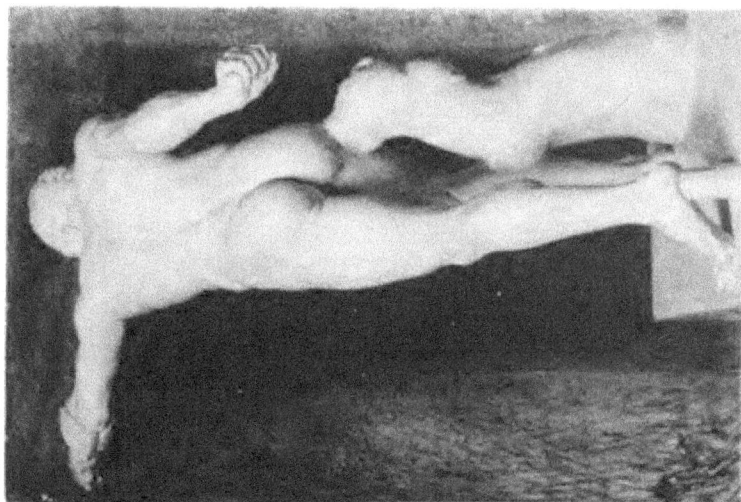

BRONZE MEDAL. **Chalk Drawing of Figure
from the Antique.** CHARLES D. WARD.
ROYAL COLLEGE OF ART

SILVER MEDAL. JOHN J. ROBERTSHAW.
ROYAL COLLEGE OF ART.

Chalk Drawing of Figure from the Antique.

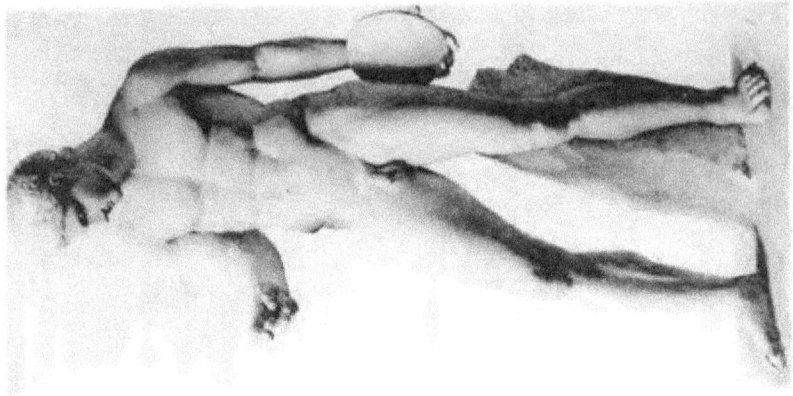

SILVER MEDAL.   Chalk Drawing of Figure from the Cast.   WM. N. M. OWEN,
DUBLIN.

Chalk Drawing of Drapery arranged on an Antique Figure.

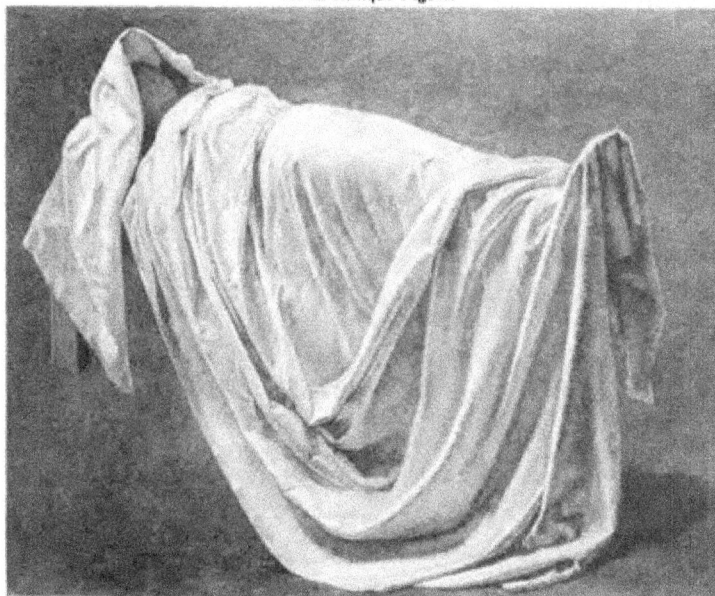

Chalk Drawing of Drapery.

DESIGN FOR A CHURCH

SILVER MEDAL.

Design for a Church.

ROLAND D. RAWCLIFFE,
ROYAL COLLEGE OF ART

Modelled Figure Group.

Ruby W. Levick.
Royal College of Art.

Design for a Piano Front.
SHEET 51.

GEORGE MONTAGUE ELLWOOD.
HOLLOWAY.

GOLD MEDAL.

GEORGE MONTAGUE ELLWOOD, HOLLOWAY.

Design for Mantel Decoration and Doorway.

GOLD MEDAL.

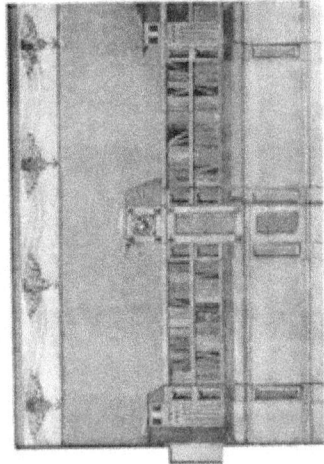

Design for the Interior Decoration of a Library. ARTHUR H. BAXTER, LEICESTER.

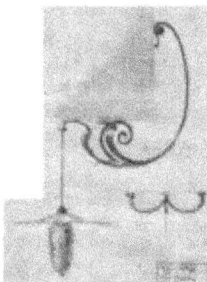

GOLD MEDAL.   Design for the Interior Decoration of a Library.   ARTHUR H. BAXTER, LEICESTER.

56

GOLD MEDAL.   OFFLOW SCATTERGOOD,
                                        BIRMINGHAM.

Designs for Tapestry.

57

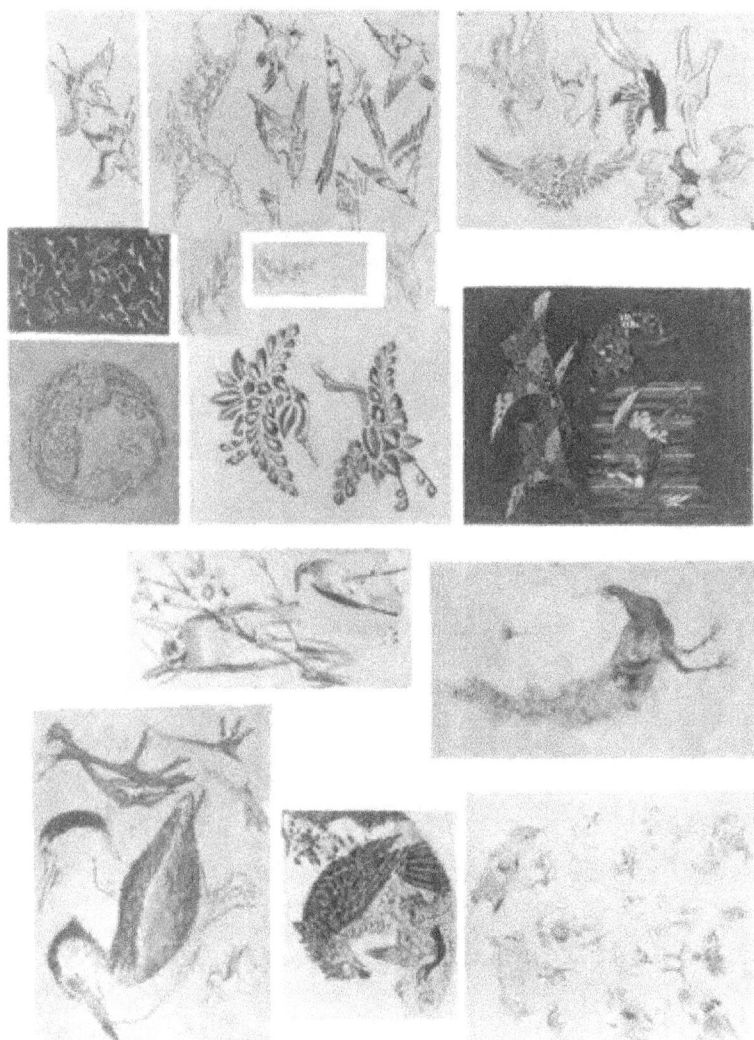

Studies of Historic Styles of Ornament.

CHARLES A. EVA,
ROYAL COLLEGE OF ART.

GOLD MEDAL.

GOLD MEDAL.　　　　Design for Wall Paper and Frieze.　　　　HELENA R. DOW, GLASGOW.

SILVER MEDAL.   Designs for Book Illustrations.   SUNDERLAND ROLLINSON,
SCARBOROUGH.

SILVER MEDAL. **Design for a Lace Collar.** GEORGINA WILLS. CROYDON.

SILVER MEDAL. **Designs for Lace Scarf Lappets.** ALICE JACOB. DUBLIN.

61

GOLD MEDAL.   Modelled Design for Embossed Wall Filling.   JOSIAH CONNOR, SALFORD.

ALICE MARY APPLETON,
HAMMERSMITH.

Designs based on a Flowering Plant,
to fill given spaces.

GRACE MEANS.

Design for a Damask Table Cloth.   ILLINGWORTH VARLEY, MACCLESFIELD.

SILVER MEDAL.

BRONZE MEDAL.   GEORGE MONTAGUE ELLWOOD, HOLLOWAY.

Designs for Book Covers.

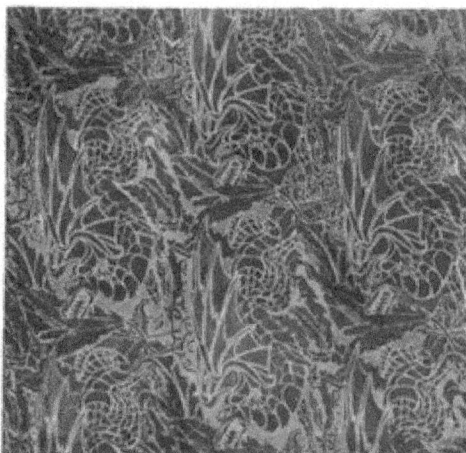

SILVER MEDAL. **Stencil Design.** CHRISTINA STEVENS GRAHAM. NEWCASTLE-ON-TYNE (DURHAM COLLEGE).

SILVER MEDAL. **Stencil Design.** ELIZABETH DAVIES, NEWCASTLE-ON-TYNE (DURHAM COLLEGE).

Design for a Stencilled Frieze and Filling. GEOFFREY ALAN BAKER, CANTERBURY

Studies of Historic Styles of Ornament.

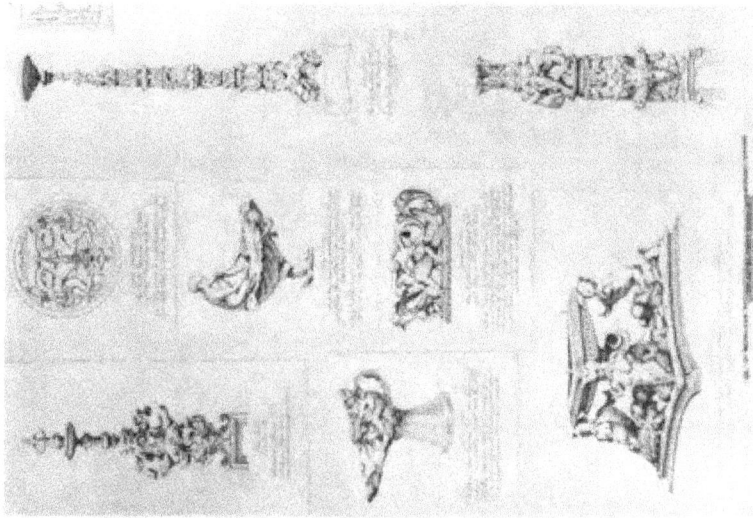

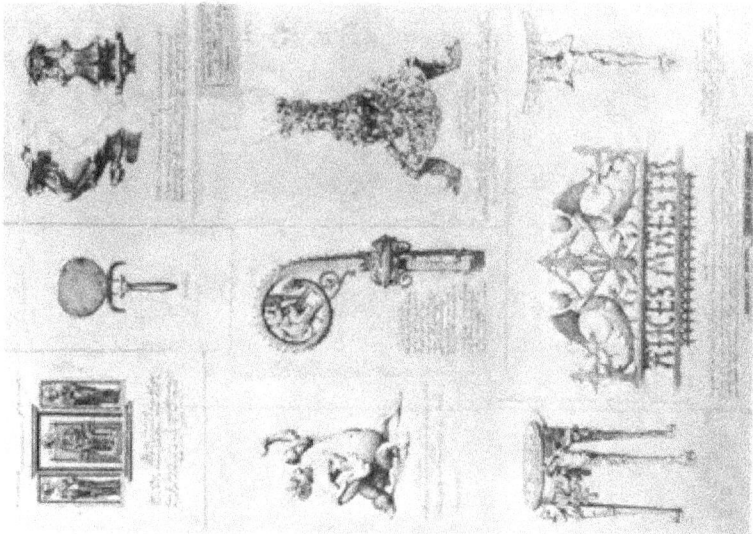

Studies of Historic Styles of Ornament.

Designs for Book Covers and a Lady's Belt.

Mary G. Houston,
Royal College of Art.

Stencil Design. ELIZABETH HILDREDS NAYLOR, NEWCASTLE-ON-TYNE (DURHAM COLLEGE).
SILVER MEDAL.

Stencil Design. META LONGDEN, NEWCASTLE-ON-TYNE (DURHAM COLLEGE).
SILVER MEDAL.

SILVER MEDAL.   Modelled Design for the Decoration of a Pulpit.   CHARLES ANDREWS SHEEHAN,
KENSINGTON SCHOOL, BRISTOL.

Silver Medal.

Modelled Design for a Mace.

Albert A. Pashley,
Sheffield.

Silver Medal.

Modelled Design for a Mace.

Oxar Ramsdon,
Sheffield.

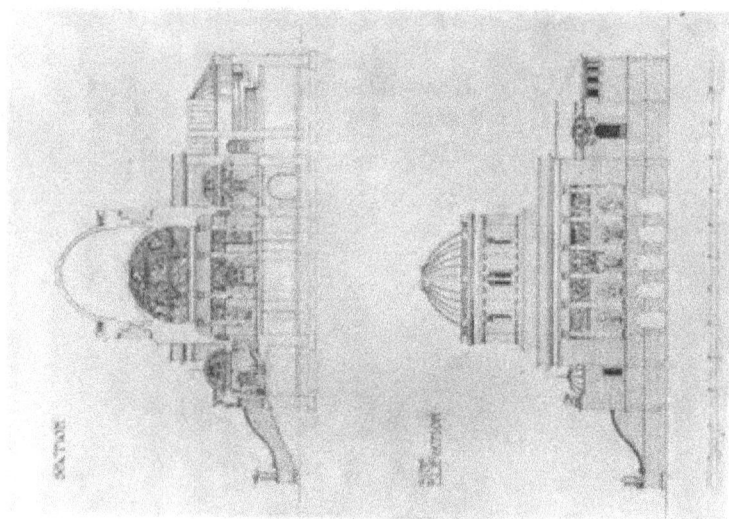

SILVER MEDAL.   **Design for a Small Art Department.**   DONALD M. STODDART, GLASGOW.

73

Designs for the Decoration of a Music Room.

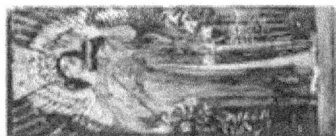

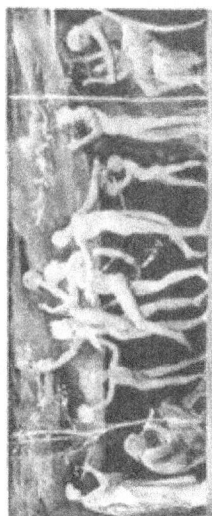

Henry E. Crocket.
Royal College of Art.

Silver Medal.

SILVER MEDAL.   Figure Design.   VIOLET M. HOLDEN,
BIRMINGHAM.

SILVER MEDAL.   Design for a Wall Paper.   HERBERT D. RICHTER,
BATH.

SILVER MEDAL. Foliage Modelled from Nature. EDWARD CYRIL POMEROY, KENSINGTON SCHOOL, BRISTOL.

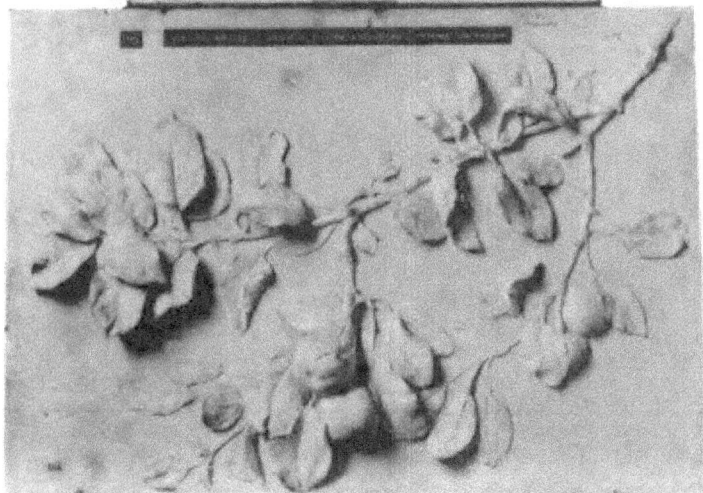

SILVER MEDAL. Fruit and Foliage Modelled from Nature. ARTHUR HULME LONGMORE, STOKE-ON-TRENT.

BRONZE
MEDAL.   Design for Wall Paper.   WILLIAM F. BROWN,
GLASGOW.

SILVER
MEDAL.   Design for Wall Paper.   WILLIAM F. BLAGG,
CHELSEA.

Design for Lace Scarf Lappets and Handkerchief.

BRONZE MEDAL.   WILLIAM ALBERT BENNETT, SALFORD.

Chalk Study of Drapery arranged on an Antique Figure.

BRONZE MEDAL.   JOSEPH OLDER, ROYAL COLLEGE OF ART.

Chalk Study of Drapery.

BRONZE MEDAL.   WILLIAM ALBERT BENNETT, SALFORD.

Chalk Study of Drapery arranged on an Antique Figure.

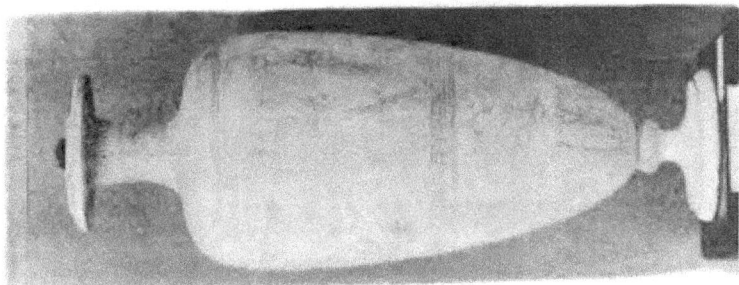

BRONZE MEDAL. **Modelled Design for a Vase.** GEORGE J. CARTER. WORCESTER ART SCHOOL.

BRONZE MEDAL. **Modelled Design for a Clasp.** ELEANOR M. MERCER. ROYAL COLLEGE OF ART.

Design for the Decoration of a Sundial.

HERBERT J. HAMPSHIRE,
ROYAL COLLEGE OF ART.

BRONZE MEDAL.

DESIGN FOR AN EARTHENWARE PLATE.

SECTION.

SILVER
MEDAL.

Design for an
Earthenware Plaque.

GEORGE CARTLIDGE,
HANLEY.

BRONZE MEDAL.   Design for a Tapestry Panel.   FLORENCE A. BIRCH.
WEST BROMWICH.

BRONZE MEDAL.   Design for a Book Cover.   EDGAR GEORGE PERMAN.
WESTMINSTER.

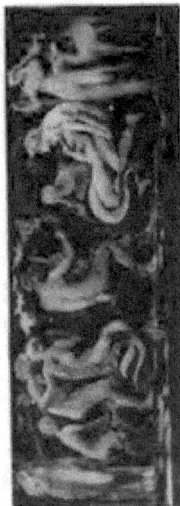

SILVER MEDAL.   **Design for the Decoration of a Music Room.**   HENRY E. CROCKET. ROYAL COLLEGE OF ART.

SILVER MEDAL.   **Design for Printed Muslin.**   FRANCIS JONES. BATTERSEA.

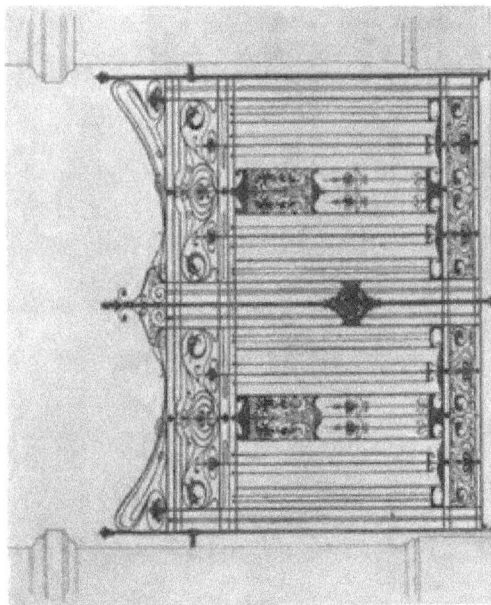

BRONZE MEDAL. Design for Wrought Iron Gates. THOMAS D. BRYAN, KENSINGTON SCHOOL, BRISTOL.

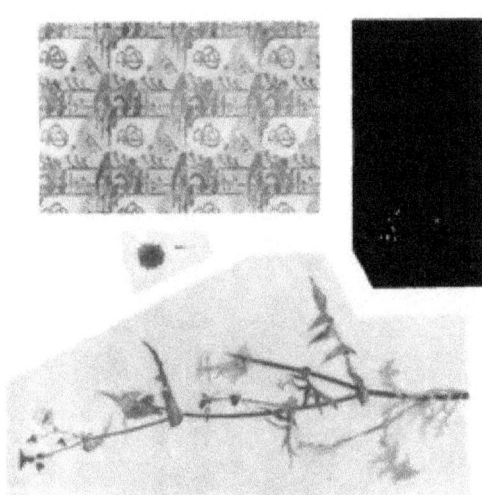

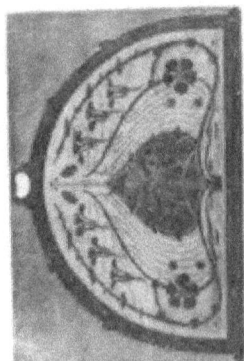

Designs based on a Flowering Plant.

Designs based on a Flowering Plant.

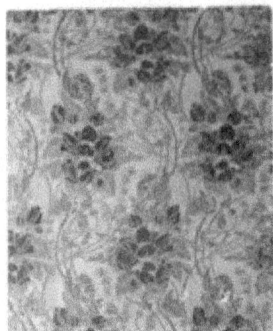

Designs based on a Flowering Plant. ALFRED JEFFERSON,
BRADFORD TECHNICAL COLLEGE.

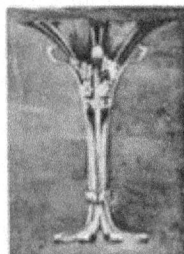

Designs based on a Flowering Plant. EDITH JAMES,
BRADFORD TECHNICAL COLLEGE.

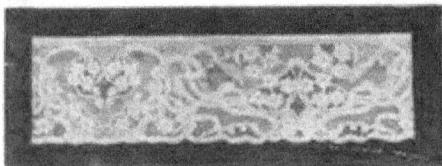

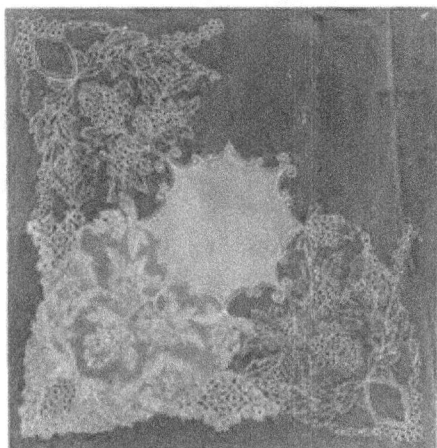

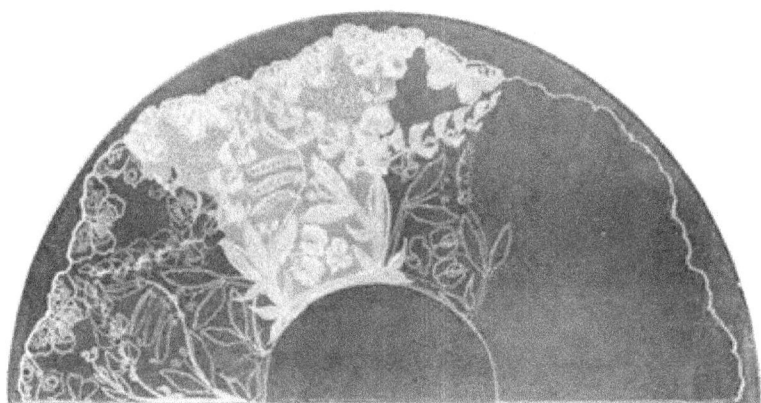

Designs for Lace Handkerchief and Fan. C. ANNIE M. CLAY, WEST BROMWICH.

Designs for Damask Table Cloths.

Design for a Damask Table Cloth.

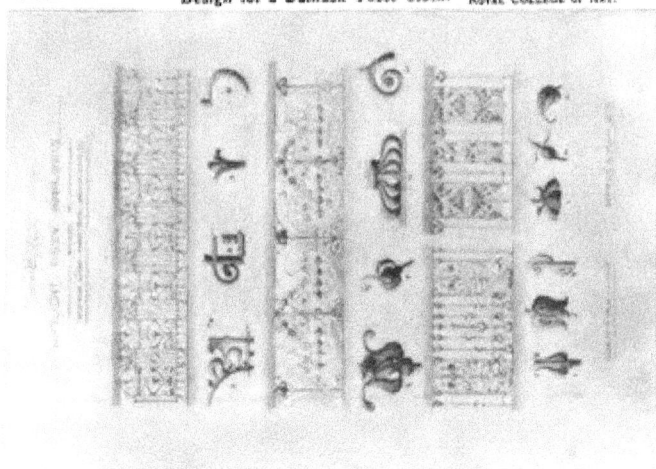

Designs for Wrought Iron Railings.

SILVER MEDAL.   Design for a Carpet.   JOHN W. WADSWORTH,
MACCLESFIELD.

BRONZE MEDAL.   Design for Tapestry Hanging.   JENNIE H. WOOD,
MANCHESTER.

Designs for Damask Serviettes. HELENA APPLEYARD, SCARBOROUGH

BRONZE MEDAL.   CHARLES H. LAWFORD, LEICESTER.
GOLD MEDAL.   WILLIAM BRYAN BINNS, BRISTOL (QUEEN'S ROAD).

Model of Figure from the Nude.   Model of Figure from the Nude.

BRONZE METAL. Design for a **Gesso Panel.** ROBERT P. GOSSOP.
HOLLOWAY.

94

Silver Medal   Frank F. Marriott
New Cross

Modelled Design for a
Drinking Fountain.

Bronze Medal   Frank F. Marriott
New Cross

Modelled Design for a
Bronze Electric Bell Push

NATIONAL BOOK PRIZE.

Design for a Music Cabinet.

FRANK P. MARRIOTT.
NEW CROSS.

BRONZE MEDAL.

Designs for Book Covers.

FRANK P. MARRIOTT.
NEW CROSS.

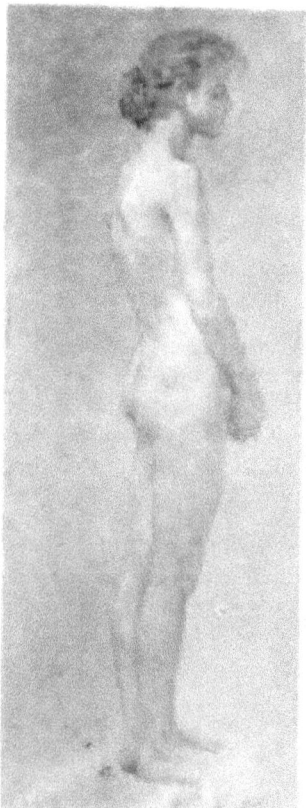

Bronze Medal.   Albert E. P. Jackson.
Holloway.

**Chalk Drawing of Figure
from the Nude.**

Bronze Medal.   Edith Piper.
Holloway.

**Chalk Drawing of Figure
from the Nude.**

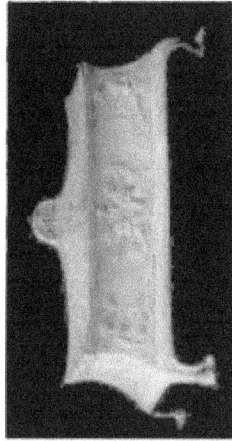

Modelled Design for a Wrought Silver Casket.

Modelled Design for Metal Work.

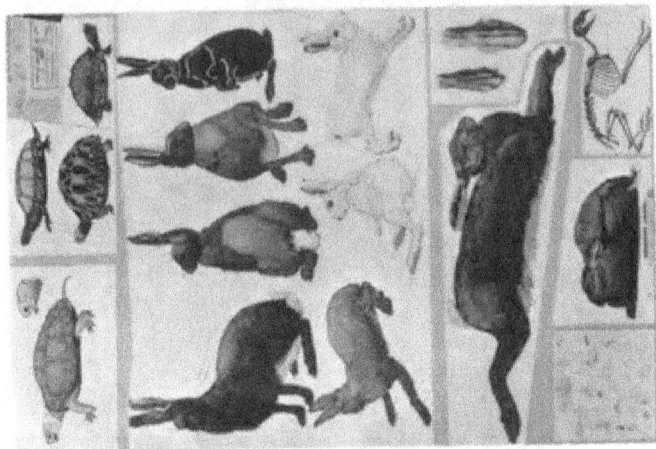

Natural History Specimens treated for Design.

SILVER MEDAL.　　　　JOHN CONWAY BLATCHFORD,　　BRONZE MEDAL.　　　　STANLEY N. BABB.
　　　　　　　　　QUEEN'S ROAD, BRISTOL.　　　　　　　　　ROYAL COLLEGE OF ART.

Modelled Figure Group.　　　　　　　　**Modelled Study of Drapery.**

Bronze Medal.

Katherine M. Cooze,
New Cross.

Design for Silver Sugar Basin, Sifters and Spoons.

SILVER MEDAL.

WILLIAM ALBERT BENNETT,
SALFORD.

Modelled Design for a Jar and Cover.

SILVER MEDAL.

Modelled Design for a Casket.

EDITH A. COWLES,
BIRMINGHAM.